# THE QUICK GUIDE TO CO-PARENTING AFTER DIVORCE

## THREE STEPS TO YOUR CHILDREN'S HEALTHY ADJUSTMENT

LISA GABARDI, PH.D.

Lisa Gabardi, Ph.D., LLC
Licensed Psychologist
Beaverton, Oregon 97006-7374
(503) 629-0272
Fax (503) 617-0475

www.gabardi.com

*To Mom and Dad for accepting their parenting differences, raising me well, and loving me, no matter what.*


*For my children, with love, for their patience, flexibility, acceptance and resilience in adjusting to reconfigured families.*

# A Note about Word Choice

For readability purposes only, I have used the word "children" instead of "child" throughout the book. Please consider these words to be interchangeable . Also, I have used the masculine noun or pronoun for descriptive purposes only. Father/Mother, son/daughter, and he/she can be used interchangeably.

*All characters and situations in this book represent common situations that are composites of family circumstances I have encountered. No examples are based upon any actual person, living or dead.*

# This book is not a replacement for therapy or other professional guidance

This book is intended as a general guide and for informational purposes only. It is not meant to offer specific guidance for your personal circumstances nor is it a substitute for specific research findings or legal, financial, psychotherapy, or other professional assistance. If you believe that you could benefit from such assistance, please consider seeking competent professional services.

# CONTENTS

# INTRODUCTION
## WHY MAKE TIME TO READ THIS?

One of the top concerns of parents contemplating a divorce is how the divorce will affect their children. There have been many studies done and many books written on this topic. I reference information from some of my favorite books on the topic in this guide. While I know that parents worry terribly about how divorce will affect their children and want their children to have the best chances of success, I also know that, on a practical level, parents during the divorce process are so busy and overwhelmed by their own feelings, the details involved in all of the changes, and with gathering and processing information to finalize a divorce, that they likely have precious little time to devote to reading the best full-length books on the topic. Since your time and resources are limited, I've distilled the best information from the experts on what makes for healthy divorce adjustment for your children and for you.

Divorce is a major stress and loss for all members of the family. As with any major stress or loss, those affected will have feelings and reactions that require soothing, support, and time to heal. Just as we are able to recover and heal from other stressful events or losses in our lives, so too can your children heal from divorce. I'm going to review some key steps you can take to facilitate the adjustment process for your children. The message I want to give you is that it's possible for your children to heal, adjust well, and have a thriving childhood in a new family organization of two households. And, in the process of giving the best to your children, you may find that you have also given yourself some important gifts, such as self regulation, cooperation, courage, persistence, responsibility taking, respect, and ultimately resilience.

*So, I think you will want to read this because…*

1. You want the best for your children and want to minimize their pain and suffering and help them to heal and adjust.

2. You want and deserve to heal from the pain and loss, learn from the experience, move on, and build a hopeful, positive future for yourself and your family.

3. Practicing the guidance in this book offers an opportunity for personal growth and character-building and strengthening that could contribute to your overall health, happiness, well-being, and self confidence and to thriving in other challenging situations and goals you set for yourself.

Bottom-line summary of the research: (Emery, Gold, Thayer & Zimmerman)

*Parents' relationship to each other and their relationships to their children are very significant factors affecting children's general well-being and adjustment. Post-divorce, this continues to be true, just more difficult to achieve.*

*Children do best during and after divorce when their parents are able to minimize the conflict between them and cooperatively provide consistent availability, love, routines, and limits.*

*One of the most important things you can do to give your child the best chance of adjusting well to this significant life event is to minimize the conflict you have with their other parent.*

If you want to help your children successfully adjust to the divorce—and what parent doesn't—the three steps I outline in this book are likely to be the most important steps you can take to do just that. I keep this book short and simple so that you will actually have time to read it, digest it, and refer back to it again and again without feeling overwhelmed by information. But, please take note: While this book is short and sweet, the steps outlined are anything but easy. Controlling the conflict between you and your children's other parent means managing your own feelings so they are not driving your behavior; especially since your behavior toward him, and your parenting is the key to your children's post-divorce success. It is a tall parenting order under the best of circumstances and even more so during the stressful period during and following your divorce. I want to help you realize that you can do it and I want to share some key steps to getting there.

But first, if you aren't convinced yet that this brief book is a good investment of your very limited time and energy, consider reading on about my story, about why I so believe the importance of what I am going to tell you. It's not just because of my professional background, it's because I've lived through how hard it can be to do what I'm going to suggest you do and because I now have a decade of living it to see what rewards can be reaped.

## IMAGINING FUTURE FAMILY SCENARIOS AND A SCENE FROM MY STORY

I got divorced when my two sons were young. I felt those feelings: overwhelmed, scared, hurt, and angry. I didn't trust or like my ex, my sons' father. I had the same strong feelings and the natural worries about my children and how they would adjust as most parents in the wake of divorce do. To make it worse, I knew the divorce literature and knew clinically that kids suffer when their divorced parents can't get along. I knew what I needed to do for my children—and for myself. Doctor, heal thyself; walk the talk. Wow.

It was quite humbling to discover just how hard it was to do the things I had advised others to do on countless occasions. It was initially very difficult. I discovered, in a very real and personal way, just how challenging it can be to keep strong feelings from interfering in what we know to be best. I stumbled often, but persisted, keeping my eye on the prize (getting to a better place and doing my best on behalf of my boys) and getting lots of support.

For the most part, the boys' dad and I were able to do it. We both worked very hard at it and it took time. Feelings for each other aside; there was no doubt that we both loved our sons very much. We caused the loss of their intact family and the related pain, suffering, and losses for them. The least we could do was minimize their ongoing suffering by resisting fighting each other.

The first year or two of separation and divorce were the hardest because that's when the hurt and anger were most intense. A little more than two years after the divorce was final, crisis struck—our youngest son was in a terrible motor vehicle accident. I received the call that he was on a life flight to pediatric intensive care. This is the type of call that every parent fears and never wants to receive.

I was met by their dad's new wife in the ER since she was the first to arrive at the hospital. My son's father and I spent the night with him in his intensive care room. Can you imagine the scene? There's nothing like wondering if your child might die to reorder your priorities. In those moments, all I could think about was my son and willing him to heal and be all right again. I remember thinking to myself, *There's no room for negative energy here.* I tried to stay focused on my son, my role as his mother, and what was really important.

As helpless as I felt, I made it my job to send all of my energy to my son and his healing. I harnessed every ounce of strength and hope I could manage and directed it toward him. Old negative feelings about my son's father and the divorce were quite low on the list of priorities for my attention. While he was in the hospital and during the weeks afterward at both of our homes recovering, our son needed his family, his whole family, his mom and his dad, along with extended family members and close friends. He needed as much love, support, and positive energy as he could get from us. I believe with my whole heart and mind that the enormous love, positive energy, and togetherness he was able to feel from all around him helped him to heal as miraculously and quickly as he did.

Can you imagine what that scene might have turned into if my son's father and I still regularly engaged in angry bickering and blame or positioning for control? If we weren't able to keep our private feelings separate from our parenting and as far away from our children as possible? What if, two years after the divorce, we were still unable to make cooperative decisions about what was in our children's best interest? What might it have been like for me and for my son if his father and I couldn't be in the same room together?

I've often thought about that, and I'm so grateful and thankful we made the efforts we made. I wouldn't wish that experience on my worst enemy. And though it's hard to imagine the situation being any worse than it was; it could've been magnitudes worse if my son's father and I couldn't and didn't do our best to work things out together.

Imagine the relationship you now have with your child's mother or father. How would a hospital scene look? What would your child want from his mom and dad as he lay in that hospital bed? Could you give it to him? I want to help you to be able to do that, for all of the critical moments in life for you and your child in the years to come.

Now, imagine that some of those critical life moments aren't so dramatic. They're the day-to-day life moments we cherish as parents, such as the soccer game, getting ready before the big dance, or the school conference. Don't let these moments be tarnished by anger, loyalty tugs of war, pain and suffering, or missed altogether because you can't get along. And please, don't let it take a life-threatening crisis to reorder your priorities. Our children need as much love, support, and positive energy as possible from those who love them every day, not just in times of crisis.

I hope that you allowed yourself to truly imagine my story and potential future stories in your own life. I share it in the hopes of helping you as a parent, while your divorce wounds are still fresh and it's so hard to imagine other feelings and another future, to really consider how you want to move forward.

 Please consider what possible positive future is available to you and your family. I want to appeal to your wounded, hurting, post-divorce heart and redirect it to the love you have for your children, what you want for your children, the moments in your life that you'll want to be with your children, and how you'll want to be with them.

There will be occasions that you will not want to miss because you can't be in the same room with their mother or father. Do you want to show up at some happy, or God forbid, scary or unhappy event and have your child worried about how Mom and Dad are going to get along or if they are going to have to deal with the tension of the two of you subtly or not so subtly continuing some long ago battle in addition to managing whatever stressful event just occurred? Of course you don't want that. What parent would? So, what are you going to do about it? The time to start is now, and I'm going to help you learn what you can do about it.

If you picked up this book, you're probably embarking on the roller coaster ride of the divorce process. Or perhaps you have been divorced for some time and continue to find yourself locked in battle with your children's father, or you're worried about your children and how they're adjusting. If you're still reading this, you probably want something better for yourself and your children.

In the early months and perhaps even years during and following the divorce, there can still be fresh, strong feelings. Negative interactions with the other parent open old wounds and reconfirm old biases and negative perceptions. While your feelings may be understandable, tensions, icy distance, and/or outright fights are not good for you and are definitely not good for your kids.

Perhaps it's early enough in the process that it's hard for you to imagine a time in the future when you're interacting well with someone who, for the moment, is a source of frustration and pain. Perhaps you imagine having as little to do with this person as you possibly can. Or perhaps you feel justified in how you treat them after all the pain and suffering they have caused you.

We can't know the future, but I can tell you, you probably can't now imagine all the ways you may need to come together with your children's other parent in the years to come. You may be thinking high school or college graduations or a wedding. Have you imagined how you'd like the occasion to be? More importantly, have you imagined how your child would want it to be?

And beyond how your child wants and needs the interactions to be, have you allowed yourself to imagine a future time when you're past how you're feeling right now, in a better place emotionally and with your life? Have you imagined a future in which you interact well and without strong feelings or drama with your children's father? I am writing this to tell you that it's possible. It's possible and you play a starring role in building that potential future.

I'm familiar with the research and I have years of clinical experience with people going through divorce. I've also lived it. I understand divorce from clinical, empirical, and personal angles. I know what the research says works and I've tried to walk the talk. I know how hard it is to do; I know how important it is to do, and I know it can work and is well worth the effort.

# STEP 1
## MANAGE YOUR FEELINGS

### PARENT'S FEELINGS AND CHILDREN'S FEELINGS ARE SEPARATE

Mistrust, disappointment, confusion, guilt, rejection, hurt, sadness, anger—these are common feelings as a marriage ends and the divorce process begins. They're understandable and natural feelings to have, yet when acted out with the other parent, they undermine the effectiveness of your parenting relationship. Hurt, angry feelings and mistrust fuel guardedness, defensiveness, blame, and resistance. These feelings distort our perceptions and make interacting, understanding, and compromise difficult. Acting on these feelings promotes more mistrust, hurt, anger, and bad feelings and bad faith.

Sometimes parents distort their own feelings by projecting their feelings onto their children or assume their children have the same feelings they do. You're all experiencing loss; however, you and your children's feelings about the divorce are not necessarily the same. And your children's feelings about their other parent are certainly not the same as your feelings toward the other parent. Commingling them robs your children of their own experience and often does so at the other parent's expense.

A common example might be when Jane comes home from a visit to her dad's with a stomach ache or complaining about the time there. If you've immediately jumped to the conclusion that Jane isn't happy with her father and the visit or that her father's behavior is the reason Jane is unhappy, then you're in danger of assuming that your angry feelings about Jane's father and criticism of how he parents Jane is what Jane is feeling. Beware! You've just used your own feelings to filter the information about your child's experience. You haven't checked with Jane as to her reasons for what she said.

And, even if Jane says something to reinforce your negative perceptions of her father ("Dad was mean to me"), be cautious as to your interpretations. Maybe Dad stuck to your agreed-upon consequences for behavior and Jane was unhappy with the consequences, rather than what Dad did wrong. Maybe he did something right and Jane is just being a normal kid and complaining about it. But, if you're angry and hurt and looking for a reason to blame her father, you might not give him the benefit of the doubt and consider that maybe Jane is just being a kid (and maybe complains to her Dad about *you*). You might use what Jane says to justify your feelings. At that point, it's no longer about helping Jane with her feelings or getting to the bottom of what's going on for Jane—you've let it become about how you feel.

In the wake of divorce, a parent's feelings often can be so strong that those feelings get in the way of clearly seeing our children, their needs, experiences of the divorce, and their feelings. And, of course, no parent is objective about their own children. The responsible parent must take care of themselves and their own feelings sufficiently to keep them from getting in the way of having any emotional energy or reasoned approach to taking care of their children.

# COPING WITH STRONG FEELINGS

To parent well and give your children what they need to adjust to this divorce, you need to work on some Herculean tasks: manage the intensity of your personal feelings, cope with the complicated feelings and losses of the divorce, and do this separately from interactions with your former spouse. I don't mean to suggest that you aren't entitled to those important feelings or that you can't express them. I'm suggesting that expressing those personal feelings are no longer part of the contract you share with your former spouse. Your feelings may be about him, the marriage, or the divorce, and it might *feel* like the thing to do, but that doesn't mean it *would* be the best thing to do.

The painful truth is that you're no longer married. Your feelings and experiences were important to discuss during the marriage as part of that intimate relationship. With the end of the marriage relationship comes the end of that sharing. You'll be forging a different relationship with your ex (more on that later) that doesn't involve that level of personal connection. While a very difficult transition to make, it's a necessary and wise one.

In order to now be effective in attending to the needs of your shared children, you need to exert enormous personal discipline and self control to separate your strong feelings from decisions and interactions about and on behalf of your children. The more you manage your strong feelings, the less they'll control you and the less they'll drive your decision-making and actions; decisions and actions that can affect you and your children for years. You could be living out the potentially regrettable effects of your pain or anger long after you're done feeling that pain or anger. I don't think you want that. And, I know that your children don't want that.

Create an imaginary shield or bubble that separates you and your feelings from your ex-spouse and that also protects you from his feelings. Practice some level of emotional distancing or disengagement when interacting with your ex-spouse. This may initially require 'fake it 'til you make it' compartmentalizing and rigid emotional boundaries. Practice will help this feel less strange and unnatural over time.

Think about other situations in your life when you have successfully kept your feelings to yourself and managed to stay relatively calm to handle an important situation. Perhaps it was at work with a boss or coworker or with personnel at a store or at the airport. Most of us can recall a time we kept our cool under duress. Be proud of that ability and remind yourself you already possess some of the skills you need.

Imagine the other parent is your business partner and you have to be polite, have business-like conversations, and work together or your business will go bankrupt. You'll be digging deep into your resolve and strength of character to make it work. You may not succeed every time, but no one is accomplished at a task from the beginning. We all need practice and make mistakes as we learn. Successful people practice a lot and don't give up. The taste of hard-won successes and personal goals met is sweet. You can do this!

Remember, your feelings are understandable. They deserve your attentive self-care and soothing so you can heal. However, that doesn't mean it's wise to act on them impulsively the moment you first experience them. How things seem now can be distorted by the intensity of the feelings. It's in your interest and definitely in your children's interests for you to get a handle on these strong feelings, both for your own well-being and especially for the interactions you need to have with your children's other parent.

# PERSONAL INVENTORY

Take a personal inventory and take your emotional temperature. Increase your awareness about when you're becoming emotional, how you feel it, and how "hot" or intense the feelings are. Ask yourself the following:

*Are you tense, tight, numb, heavy?*

*Breathing shallowly?*

*Heart racing?*

*Sick to your stomach?*

*Clenching muscles?*

*Feeling flush?*

*Scowling?*

*What are you thinking? Are you bracing for the worst? Preparing for a fight? Focusing on how unfair this all is?*

Take note and see this as a sign to check yourself and slow down. Remind yourself that it's understandable that you're tense around this person. Maybe they've been a source of pain or mistrust and you perceive danger around them. On the other hand, there's also another side that might be obscured. This is someone who also loves your children. You both want what's best for them, although you may differ on what you believe to be best and how to get there. You share common ground that is sacred and worth fighting together to protect rather than fighting against each other and tearing it apart.

Balancing these perceptions may help you reduce the danger signals about this other person. There is no need to deny or minimize your feelings, they're real and understandable. It's

13

beneficial to check the distortion level of the feelings to create a fair and balanced view and control your ability to manage the feelings and their expression. Like I said, you're entitled to your feelings, but care for your feelings separately from the other person; either on your own or with a trusted friend, family member, or professional. You'll benefit from creating a bit of time and space between yourself and these feelings for the purposes of interacting with the other parent.

## SELF-SOOTHING STRATEGIES

The first thing I recommend you do when you know you're emotional is to slow down enough to get a handle on it and engage your thinking. If we can slow down, we can create a buffer zone between the initial feeling and impulsive reactions. *Breathing slowly and deeply can be a good first step.* Breathing is always with us and we can regulate and change it without too much effort. It can have the effect of slowing down our body and sending the signal to our body that we're in a state of rest, rather than fight-flight. This is helpful, because our body in fight-flight sets a stage for panicky or angry interactions that will do more harm than good.

Sure, in the short-term it can feel good to get something off your chest, give them what they have coming to them (in your mind), not take it anymore, etc. However, it will not serve your long-term interests involving the ongoing interactions and negotiations you'll have with this person. It can be helpful to allow some buffer time to move from our impulsive emotional brain to our rational, thinking, and future-planning brain. For example, someday you may want to switch parenting days, or ask for a few extra vacation days, or a different holiday, and you'll wish you had set the stage for cooperation with this person. And it will definitely not serve your children to feed or fuel conflict with this person who your children love and need in their lives.

While slowing your breathing, think of other soothing activities to help you feel better. Engage all of your senses and notice which strategies for coping with these strong feelings work best and you enjoy most. Consider music, enjoyable smells, or looking at beautiful images. Consider splashing your face with water, a warm or cool healthy drink, muscle relaxation or enjoyable exercise, or hugs or cuddling with a pet. Perhaps you'll find some peace or release in talking to a friend or journaling or laughing at something or doing a favorite activity. Try as many of these as you can and repeat your favorites often.

## THINKING STRATEGIES

Monitoring your thinking will also be an important part of the calming-down strategy. Catastrophic, rigid, or angry thinking can worsen how you feel. Reviewing negative events or interactions or your injuries over and over in your mind magnifies the original feelings associated with the event and makes it seem bigger and worse. Reviewing old business will not help you develop a new business relationship with your children's other parent.

Allow yourself a limited length of time (say 30 minutes) to lick your wounds and indulge your injuries. Apply the soothing strategies liberally. Limit the time to limit the damage. Focus on soothing and nurturing yourself through your pain. Then, practice symbolically putting it in a container on a shelf and moving on with the tasks at hand in your day. This practice can facilitate the notion of compartmentalizing, drawing boundaries, and shifting focus to the present.

On a small scale, you'll be practicing what will be necessary to your healing on a large scale. You can't change the past and you can't change your children's other parent, but you can learn from the past, change yourself, and move forward differently by influencing your co-parenting interactions in a positive direction.

Challenge negative thinking and replace it with realistic, positive thinking that promotes acknowledging your strengths and considering alternatives and possibilities. Try to stop yourself from using language that includes "should," "always," or "never." These words encourage extreme and negative views. Challenge blame and guilt thinking.

Instead, consider each person's contribution (including yours) to the problem and the solutions available. Remind yourself of difficult situations and people you've dealt with successfully in the past and how you were able to do that. Remind yourself that painful feelings don't last forever and that you've survived and thrived through other setbacks in life.

Remind yourself of what you're thankful for in your life. I know that sometimes we can hit very rough patches in our lives when we look around and it's hard to find areas of our life going well that we're thankful for, but look harder and think more broadly. I know I've sometimes joked that I can be thankful I don't have an inoperable brain tumor and two weeks to live or I have shelter from the elements or we have potable water to drink and food to eat. And then, noting the gallows humor, I've added that I'm thankful that I still have my sense of humor! Most importantly, use thinking that reminds yourself of your larger parenting purpose and what your children need from you.

Also, challenge yourself if you only have negative things to say about your children's other parent. Remember, you once loved this person and chose to be with him, he must have had some redeeming qualities because you're not totally crazy and self defeating. Consider some of his positive qualities and ways that he adds value to your children's lives.

Also, remind yourself about what is both within and outside of your control. Who he is, his lifestyle, values, and the ways he chooses to parent are all outside of your control. This can be scary and difficult, but important to accept. There's a difference between aiming for consistency in your parenting and needing to control and have every element of your parenting and decision-making reflect what you would do. Remember, you probably didn't do everything the same way with the children when you were married. Kids understand how and when Mom and Dad do things differently and can thrive in the exposure to those different approaches (so long as those approaches are loving, reasoned, and safe, of course).

For example, my own parents couldn't have been more different in personality and parenting style. They were married until my mother's death and my father remained devoted to her memory for the rest of his days. But I received very different parenting from each of them. In fact, I often thought that if I'd been raised by two parents that were exactly like either one of them (whether they remained married or divorced) I would've been worse off. I really believe that the balance between both of their styles was good for me.

Consider that your parenting differences can be good for your kids, too. Even if you have trouble believing that, believe this—chronic conflict with the other parent about those differences is definitely not good for your children. Consider another common (and likely distorted) thought about your children's other parent—that he's the cause of the majority of the problems and conflicts between the two of you. He's probably thinking the same thing about you and you can't both be correct. Even if it would be a fair-minded and reasonable assessment that the other parent is the main cause of the conflict; you can't control him. He may be 75% of the problem, but your choices and actions can be 75% of the solution.

What you can control is changing what you feel, think, and do. Your actions alone can have a significant effect on the outcome of your interactions. Think about how good you'll feel knowing that your efforts made a positive impact on your children's adjustment to the divorce.

## THOUGHTS TO REMEMBER AND REPEAT

*"My children will suffer if I continue to engage in this conflict."*

*"My love for my children and my desire for what's best for them is greater than my negative feelings toward their mother/father right now."*

*"I said I would do anything for my children, so I'll do the hard work of being polite, respectful, and business-like to him regardless of how he behaves toward me."*

*"I am empowered by the knowledge that I'm doing right by my children."*

## GET SUPPORT

Hopefully, these steps will take you well on the way to interacting with your children's other parent in a way that is emotionally disengaged. You have understandable feelings. It's no longer appropriate to share your feelings with him. You no longer have a contract in which he's the source of comfort or care about those feelings. Take care of your feelings with someone who plays a role in your life of being caring, supportive, and gentle with your feelings. Focus on making time for support from friends and family and time to process your feelings separately from your former spouse.

A note of caution about well-meaning friends and family—they're likely to be on your side and hate to see you hurting. As a result, they're biased and not neutral parties. They may at times add fuel to your fire or directly or indirectly encourage more conflict and escalation. Identify one or two friends or family members that you respect for their maturity and for being generally fair and balanced in their views. If you don't feel you're getting enough support in processing your grief and your feelings, or if you need a more neutral or unbiased perspective, consider seeing a therapist. Obtaining support, in whatever forms work best, is an important component to coping effectively with your feelings. Coping with your feelings effectively will help you feel more in control of yourself because your feelings won't be driving your behavior. You'll be more able to avoid feelings that undermine parenting discussions and negotiations the more you're aware of your feelings and able to manage them. This is groundwork for having different interactions with your co-parent. You're beginning to separate your internal and personal experiences from the business at hand—the business of raising your children well.

# Step 2
## Transition from Marriage to the Business of Parenting

The marriage relationship ended, but your parenting relationship didn't. You both remain parents to your children, and your children still very much need both of you. This person is now your child's other parent—someone your child loves, looks up to, and will likely take after in some ways—not your spouse. You'll be moving from spouse to ex-spouse to co-parent.

To hasten this process along, please stop calling him your "ex." Call him your children's dad. Word choice is relevant. Practice the skills of interacting from step 2 consistently. Fake it 'til you make it. Do the behaviors and say the words even though you don't feel it. If you keep doing it consistently, someday you may feel it.

Realistically, grieving the end of the marriage and no longer engaging with the other parent as a spouse takes time. It's a difficult process to transition from a strong and close emotional attachment to emotional detachment. Managing your feelings and dealing with them on your own is one part of the process. Structures and boundaries for interacting are also essential.

Time is also an important ingredient. It took time for you to develop an attachment to this person, it'll take time to undo the attachment and develop a different relationship. You'll be changing the how, when, and what about aspects of relating to your former spouse, now your co-parent. This can be an awkward and difficult process. It may feel strange and uncomfortable, but believe me, new interactions that are different and uncomfortable can be better than comfortably familiar but unpleasant and painful.

## A New Business Relationship

You may be asking yourself, "If I don't have positive feelings right now for this person and it's harmful to my kids to have negative feelings toward this person, then what do I have toward this person?" Good question. I encourage people to aim eventually for neutral feelings (not highly positively or negatively charged), but in the short term, I encourage you to consider detaching from your feelings (putting them aside and keeping them separate) when interacting with the other parent, and have respect. Respect the common ground you share that you both love your children and want what's best for them. Respect the other person's role as parent to your children. Respect that your children love this person.

You both are bound by a common purpose, perhaps the most important purpose you have—loving and raising your children well. If you're like most parents, you both want to raise healthy, well-adjusted children capable of functioning independently and well in adulthood. As I mentioned earlier, a useful model of comparison would be that of business partners. Two people whose personal feelings for each other are not terribly strong, nor are they the main focus of the relationship. Their connection isn't strongly emotional or personal, yet they're bound together by an important common purpose to have a successful business. You're now in the business of raising your children. It's a business, of course, that you want to be successful.

What do I mean by a business relationship? You do not need to like this person or want to be friends. You don't even need to trust or respect the person. You do need to find ways to interact respectfully, share information necessary to the development of your children, and find creative solutions to problems. Keep in your mind the idea of productive interactions with a coworker, boss, or business associate. You probably wouldn't get overly emotional with them, even if you were having strong feelings. You would save those feelings for later and deal with them privately. You would cool down before having an important conversation. You wouldn't micro manage or run to that person with every little problem. You would likely pick your battles and try to figure out some things on your own. You may even consider trying to be extra polite or cooperative so that life at the office would be more bearable or so that the person might be more receptive to your agenda in the future. Think about this model before every interaction with your co-parent.

Another way to think about the co-parenting relationship is like extended family. You continue to be related to the other parent through your relationship with your children. You're related to someone (your child) who is related to them (kind of like in-laws). Like other extended family, we may like some of them and not others, but we will often accord them respect and find ourselves in their company through mutual associations. Since we're likely to run into these extended family members at some family events, we find ways to get along, despite not liking them very well, because someone we love loves them or because of their respected position in the family.

You can decide not to respect the person, but you need to respect their role as mother or father to the children you love and who love them. As such, you can behave in respectful, polite ways toward them. After all, you will likely be seeing them at events for the children, at the hospital, college, wedding, or funeral. Let's face it, whether the soccer field, hospital room, or church, none of these are places that merit tension or conflict—for either your children or for you.

# PREPARING FOR THE "BUSINESS MEETING"

Have regular "business meetings," to share important information, meetings that are polite, respectful, and business-like. The more conflict between you and your co-parent, the more structured and planned these meetings need to be. (Thayer & Zimmerman) Remember, your business with the other parent is now just your children, so keep the conversations focused on the children. Resist conversations about your past marriage, your relationship, or either of your personal issues. The children are where you now share common ground and common interest. Never allow your children to be the go-between and carry messages to the other parent for you. Keep your children out of your adult parenting responsibilities. Allow them to remain children. Do not let them take care of you by hiding behind them to avoid talking directly as adults with their other parent.

**Regular time (weekly is a good average) and place**

Examples:

In person at transition time if the children are conveniently not around (in another room doing homework or playing at day care)

Over the phone at a time the children are asleep or at school or activities

Via email

If your conversation happens over the phone or in person, keep the interaction time limited (30 minutes max). Set a separate time for a larger discussion (e.g., about a school or behavioral issue or changes to parenting time). The main point is to be brief, to the point, and focused on solutions and sharing relevant information.

Also, remember to keep these adult conversations separate from your children hearing them or taking any part in the conversations. These are adult conversations only, not meant for the children.

## Prepare in Advance

Do your emotional work beforehand to attend to your feelings and manage your thinking. Be prepared to be calm, respectful, and business-like.

Make an outline of the information and issues you would like to discuss in advance.

Pick your battles. Are there things you can let go? Are there things you can solve on your own without involving the other parent (e.g., can you re-arrange your schedule, can you purchase a duplicate item for your child to have at your home) as a means of eliminating an issue?

Be honest about what you might contribute to the problem or to poor communication: justifying yourself, making assumptions, blaming, manipulation, avoiding issues, resisting responsibility, interrupting, debating, considering your reality the "truth," just to name a few. Check yourself on these points before you begin and while you are talking.

## Respectful and Business-like Is

On time

Calm, neutral, and specific

Minimal focus on personal feelings and personal information

Prepared

Calls well in advance if there is a need to reschedule

# THE STRUCTURE FOR THE CONVERSATION

## 1. Relay information about the following:

• Emergencies

• Positive anecdotes and your child's successes (consider giving your child a chance to share their positive news first with their other parent)

• Medical (upcoming appointments, results of recent appointments, medicines being administered and correct dosing information, symptom updates, general health observations, school missed due to illness)

• School (important dates for upcoming events such as teacher conferences, the school play, back to school night, other special events, upcoming larger projects or tests and dates due, homework, general academic or behavioral issues or progress, any discussions or contacts with teachers or other school personnel)

• Social (important dates for upcoming events such as parties or activity events, sports and activity schedules, logistics for transportation and equipment being with the child, invitations and related RSVPs and who will be following through with that, purchasing of gifts or items needed for the event and who will be doing that)

• Home (changes to normal routines, new behaviors, discipline, especially if needed to be consistent and completed at the other home) Ex: "I notice that Jane has stopped eating vegetables at my house. Is that happening at your house?" If not, "Wow, that's great, what are you doing that's working that I could try?" If both houses are experiencing the same difficulty, is this something you think we ought to focus on? If so, "Any ideas for how you would like to approach this with Jane?" Or "How are you handling this at your house with Jane?" Ex: "I know that we agreed to nine p.m. bedtime, but last night I allowed John to stay up with me to watch the *American Idol* finale. He may be a bit tired today, I apologize for that. I plan to return to his regular bedtime next time he is at my house."

**Important Note on Logistics:** It's in your child's interest that they not miss out on social, athletic, school, or extracurricular events because they have two households. It's also in their interest to have both of their parents watch their events and cheer or praise them for their efforts if both are available to go. In that spirit, both parents should make a point to be on email, phone, or other mail listings to be notified directly by school, coaches, or other clubs about dates, times, and locations of events. Direct access to this information for each parent reduces additional communications between households and reduces the possibility of miscommunications or one parent forgetting to inform the other parent. Take responsibility for getting the information for yourself directly from the source. Schools, teams, and clubs often have email and phone listings and can accommodate more than one contact point for a family. If you're the primary contact completing information for the organization, use this as an opportunity for goodwill with the other parent. Let the other parent know that you'd be willing to provide the organization with their contact information, with their permission, so that they'll receive information from the organization directly.

## 2. Discussing parenting issues.

Be ready to use your best communication skills. *Remind yourself that you want to make your best contribution to the parenting relationship because you know that this is best for your children. You want what's best for your children.*

# COMMUNICATION SKILLS

• **Manage the intensity of your feelings** and repeat the skills from Step 1 over and over again throughout your interaction. When you feel yourself getting angry or upset, slow down, breathe, remember your purpose, 'fake it 'til you make it,' and be business-like and respectful. You will not be successful in your communication going into it full of hurt, injury, anger, or righteous indignation.

• **Perceptions: Yours and the other parent's**.
You both have sensitivities and biases. Each of you has perceptions and neither is the absolute truth; they're your viewpoints. Golden rule: if you want your perspective respected, be sure to offer the same to the other parent. Check yourself about what assumptions you may be making about the other person and the situation, consider other perspectives, and remind yourself you don't truly know the other person's motives, thoughts, or feelings. Monitor your nonverbal communication. For example, your tone of voice will change the meaning of the words you use and your body language will convey if you're open, closed, guarded, or hostile. Consider what your nonverbal demeanor would be if you were being business-like and try to replicate that as you have the conversation.

• **Humility.** Parenting is the toughest job most of us will ever love. None of us is perfect, and no one knows that

27

better than our children. Think about the gift of grace our children offer us in forgiving our missteps, mistakes, and limitations. With the exception of real abuse or neglect that requires action, check before you consider blaming to see if you're above reproach. No one's perfect, especially when it comes to the tough job of parenting. If you still believe you're justified, consider blame a communication style that will not likely produce desired results; it's likely to produce defensiveness and counter-blame and undermine any delicate progress you may have already made. Again, remember the Golden Rule—how will you want to be treated when *your* parenting choices are not "Parent of the Year" material.

• **Reasonable.** To be reasonable, you really need to incorporate all of the other suggestions above, manage your feelings, challenge your perceptions, and be humble. You can't be reasonable if you're having a lot of intense feelings, because we know that intense feelings distort our thinking and perceptions. Distorted thinking is not reasonable thinking and strong feelings that fuel impulsive actions and blurted out thoughts are not reasoned. When we're humble, we realize that our view is not the only view and that our way is not the only way, which opens up the possibility of listening to understand the other parent and consider their perspective. When we're humble, we're careful to not cast stones and blame because we know that we're not without fault and make mistakes ourselves. All of this can help us to be reasonable, fair-minded, and balanced as we communicate with the other parent.

• **Consider listening first.** You lose nothing by listening and you have the potential to gain some goodwill. Listen to try to understand the other parent's point of view. Ask clarifying questions. Summarize what you understood. Offer to reflect the feelings you believe are related to what you've heard ("It sounds very frustrating that John forgets to pack some of his baseball gear when he goes to your house.") Understanding the other point of view does not mean you agree with it; it simply means that you're willing to acknowledge and see both sides of the issue. This is critical to lowering defensiveness, building goodwill, and beginning the process of resolving a difference. Notice what listening is not—it's not listening for all of the holes in his argument or listening for what you can attack when it's your turn to talk. (e.g., "Well, you shouldn't expect John to remember on his own. You wouldn't have this problem if you just packed it for him like I do.") Listening to understand the other person is not for the purpose of debating or accusing. The goal is to understand the other parent's perspective for the purpose of doing something positive for your children, clarifying common ground, and establishing what specific issues need resolving.

• **Find common ground** around an issue that you've discussed and point it out. ("I also feel frustrated when John forgets things in transition between our homes.") Sometimes, it can be challenging to see anything you each have to say as having anything in common. Remember, if nothing else, you both want what's best for your children. You may have different perspectives on what that is, or how to get there, but your end goal is most likely the same relative to your children thriving.

• **Share observations and helpful or positive information.** Stay focused on issues related to the children. Ask the other parent their opinion and what they observe. ("I've noticed that if I ask John to stop and think before we leave the house, he does a better job of remembering things. Or, "What do you notice that works when John does remember his stuff?") Also, consider sharing anything you notice that's working or that's going well before you bring up your concerns. If possible, consider thanking your co-parent for an effort they've recently made to respond to some other issue you raised or some shared plan for parenting. ("Jane told me she couldn't watch TV the other night because she hadn't finished her homework; thanks for following through on that. It seems to be working because she knew she had to finish her homework before the TV went on today at my house.") Appreciation can go a long way toward reducing conflict.

• **Keep your concern brief and focused on the specific situation.** Talk about yourself, your feelings, your needs, and your observations. Use "I" statements for what you feel and need. ("I notice Jane hasn't had all of her soccer equipment and uniform the last few times she returned from your house. She ends up stressed about what's missing last minute and I don't have time at that point to coordinate with you about how to get it. I'd like to problem-solve with you about how we might help Jane have everything she needs when she transitions back and forth between our houses.") Avoid blame or assumptions about his motives, thoughts, or feelings. Also avoid "you" talk and global "always" or "never" statements that provoke a fight. ("You never remember to send all of Jane's soccer stuff with her and then she's upset when she comes back from your house. You just dump the problem in my lap to get to me. You know it's not my job to do all the thinking and remembering for you anymore.") You don't know what he thinks or feels and what's "not your job anymore" speaks to your marriage, not to parenting. Keep your conversations focused on parenting, on the child, and with neutral language rather than blame language. Consider focusing on solutions to specific problems. Think creatively for solutions that allow both parents to get some of what they need, always with the higher goal of what your children need.

## 3. Make requests.

Limit your requests to what's really crucial. Be sure that

requests that make your life easier or are solely for you
(switching weekends so that you can get away with girlfriends
or your new boyfriend) are lower in priority than requests that
have to do with things that are good for your child. ("Can Jane
return to my house this Sunday night so she can make brownies
with the neighbors for the Girl Scout meeting on Monday?")

If you'd like to request a change or ask for some help with
something, give the other parent as much notice as possible. If
notice is short, apologize and acknowledge that may put the
other parent in a bind. ("I apologize for the late notice. I just
learned that my boss would like me to stay late on Wednesday
to cover for her. I won't be able to leave work until six p.m.
that night to pick up John. I understand that may not work for
you.")

Remember to phrase your request as a request, not a demand.
For instance, your late work schedule does not demand the
other parent rearrange his schedule to cover your parenting
time (i.e., when you are scheduled to pick up your child). It's in
your and your children's interest that you encourage the other
parent to be willing to cooperate with you. How cooperative
would you feel if your children's dad came up to you and
declared, "I need to work late so you'll just have to rearrange
your plans and stay an extra hour with the kids." What if you
also had plans? Would you feel your time was respected? That
*you* were respected? Remember the Golden Rule. Now try it
another way. "I know this isn't your problem, and I'm happy
to look into other childcare arrangements for John; however,
if you're willing and able to stay with him for another hour on
Wednesday night, I'd greatly appreciate it. I'm sure John would
just rather stay with you, but I realize that might not work with
your plans and I might have to make other arrangements, but I
thought it best to check with you first."

Before you make a request, consider what you can offer to the
other parent that makes helping you out or agreeing to your

request also work out for them. ("I'd be happy to keep John later on Friday if that would help you out. I could pay the neighbor in advance to come to your house to stay with John until I get there if you have someplace you need to go. If you can get John to my house, I can pick up some of your carpool duty next week to make up for the extra driving.")

## 4. Thank the other parent.

Appreciation builds good will and a climate for cooperation. You want to work together because that's best for your children. You can contribute to cooperation, flexibility, and problem-solving together by using the basic rules of politeness such as "please" and "thank you." Apologies also go a long way toward mending and promoting good will. Acknowledge it when your circumstances and needs may be inconvenient to the other parent and appreciate their efforts if they help you out and honor your requests.

## 5. Briefly summarize any agreements or changes.

This is just to be sure you both have the same understanding of plans. Consider a follow-up email that summarizes any specific agreements and future plans to reduce misunderstandings or remembering different things. End the conversation with confirmation of the date and time for the next meeting.

# COMMUNICATION PITFALLS

I've just outlined a lot of ideas about how to talk to the other parent in a calm, respectful, business-like way. I also want to briefly outline a few things that are damaging to your children and undermine effective co-parenting.

## Consider the following poisonous to your family:

Say negative things about the other parent to or in front of your children.

Engage in a disagreement or confrontation in front of your children.

Yell, name-call, or curse the other parent.

Use your children to send messages to the other parent instead of communicating directly.

If it's been a real struggle for you to do some of the positive behaviors suggested, at least stop the damaging behaviors. First and foremost, do no harm. If you're struggling to learn new behaviors or to stop damaging behaviors, consider seeing a therapist for added support and assistance.

# STEP 3
## BOTH PARENTS OFFER CONSISTENCY, LOVE, AND DISCIPLINE (COORDINATED, COOPERATIVE CO-PARENTING)

## EFFECTIVE PARENTING

Children benefit from the active involvement of both parents (except in cases of serious abuse or neglect). Many clinicians and authors have suggested that effective parenting is being emotionally available and loving, while also being firm, consistent, and fair with rules, limits, and discipline. (Cline & Fay, Emery, Gottman) Whether children have one parent or two and whether they live in an intact or divorced family, children benefit from consistent, balanced parenting. Not perfect parenting—there's no such thing. But what's good for children in any family structure is especially good for children who are going through a loss of the family structure they knew and are transitioning to a new family structure.

Research also shows children do best with low conflict between parents (while married and especially after divorce). (Emery, Gold) Lowering the conflict between you and your children's other parent allows you both to communicate more regularly and effectively and work together more cooperatively. Less conflict and interpersonal road blocks between parents promotes more consistency, loving stability, and clarity about limits and consequences for your children. Offering your best parenting to your children means providing consistent love and discipline, ideally in coordination and cooperation with your children's other parent.

Divorce is a huge adjustment and loss, not just for parents, but for children as well. They're losing their intact family and at least some aspects of their routines, relationships, and living situation are changing. Their adjustment and well-being will be improved by both parents' efforts to be physically and emotionally consistently available to their children. That means children can predict and count on when they'll see each parent, that each parent is coping with their own feelings separately from them and is helping them cope as well, that each parent is cooperating with the other in order to maintain consistent routines, rules, and discipline, and that they have both parents' support in knowing they're loved by both.

## RE-ASSESS YOUR PARENTING

Use the divorce as an opportunity to assess yourself as a parent. Try to take a good, hard, non-defensive look at your parenting. Before the divorce, how would you grade yourself on consistency, loving affection, and fair and firm discipline? If you're like most parents, you have your strengths and weaknesses, as does the other parent. What aspects of being the best parent you can be for your children would you improve on?

Now that you're a single parent, are there aspects of parenting you didn't perform very much before the divorce? Perhaps you weren't the affectionate and complimentary one. Can you add more of that to your new single-parent repertoire? Perhaps you didn't render much of the discipline, or maybe you weren't great on the follow-through with the discipline. That's something you could work on now. Or maybe you weren't that involved in their day-to-day lives and care before; now you have an opportunity to be more involved on the days they're in your care. Perhaps you weren't the fun parent; now you have an opportunity to be more silly and playful. Consider it for the benefit of your children and something you can give to them during the divorce, but also consider it an investment in your own improved relationship with each of your children. Believe me, it is an investment that can pay high dividends over time.

## CONSISTENCY

Keep their mealtimes, bedtime, bedtime routines, health/ hygiene, school/activity/friend routines as similar as possible before, during, and after the divorce and across both households. Also, maintain key rules and means of discipline. Make sure these key rules are clear (both to the children and between parents) and follow through with rules and consequences consistently. It might be better for your children for you to compromise with the other parent about the rule so that it's the same in both households and then know you'll both follow it consistently, than to have two different sets of rules at each house and no consistency or follow-through from the other parent in enforcing the rules.

You each are now parenting separately, but your children will benefit from experiencing both parents also continuing to parent together on important matters. Consistency of rules across households can be most helpful to children around homework/school-related expectations, bedtime, and important rules such as curfews, screen time limitations, or off-limits activities such as when a child can have a cell phone, date, or pierce ears. Consider more minor lifestyle choices, such as whether children have dessert after dinner or a TV show they can watch as allowing each parent to make their own decisions during their parent time. Minor differences in parenting are battles not worth picking. Remember, you and the other parent most likely parented somewhat differently while you were married and your children understand how Mom and Dad are different. This isn't a problem for children when it's the small stuff; but can become a problem when parents (whether still married or after divorce) are very inconsistent on the big stuff.

It's important to also be consistent about the new routines associated with the divorce and having two households, such as transitions from Mom and Dad's houses and parenting times. It's especially important to stick to a schedule that's predictable in the early months following the divorce. Your children need to know when they will see you and that you'll be there for them at a time and place that they can count on. Your children's adjustment to new routines and schedules can happen more smoothly and occur more rapidly when the new change is applied consistently.

Consider a routine for the return home from the other parent's home that is reliable, comforting, and connecting. Be supportive of their time at the other parent's home. Show support by being interested in what they did and nonjudgmental about what they tell you. Good communication skills not only are part of effectively interacting with the other parent, they're essential to loving, authoritative parenting as well. Use those reflective listening skills. Children are more likely to talk to parents who listen well to them. Trust me, as your children get older, you're going to want them to be willing to talk to you; whether you're comfortable with what they have to say or not. Start building that relationship with your child now if you haven't already.

If you already have open communication with your children, don't let your feelings about their other parent shut it down now.

Your own distraction and fatigue, related to your divorce stress and your guilt about what's going on for your children, can contribute to undermining your consistency and availability to your child. Take care of yourself and get the support you need so you can take good care of your children. They need their parents more than ever right now. Reassure them that you're still their parent (not emotionally or physically absent, not their friend or entertainer, and especially that they're not your confidante). Muster the courage to not enter a popularity contest with the other parent; be willing to not be liked or to be out of favor.

## LOVE

• Affection: Tell them and show them you love them. Especially during the divorce, reassure them that you and their other parent have not and will not stop loving them. Other ways we can tell them we love them is by telling our children when we're proud of them or letting them know when we respect their decision. Show them physical affection if they'll allow it. If they're no longer big on physical touch, such as hugs and kisses, develop other affectionate ways to connect, such as nicknames, inside jokes, hair tussling, smiles, winks, or knowing nods.

• Availability: Reassure them that you're there for them. That means being around and available to get involved with them or to start a conversation, both at home and at their activities. Busy, working parents realistically cannot perhaps be home after school or at every recital or ball game, but you can make making the time a priority. Offer to drive them, go to practice with them, or to help with homework. I make a point to be in the same common area as my sons are (the kitchen or family room usually) doing my own thing while they do theirs just for the opportunity for one of us to comment on something the other is doing or watching or to have brief, random conversations.

• Interest: Spend time with them and sometimes be willing to let them pick the activity and the pace. Ask about their day and how they're doing. Be willing to learn about their interests, even if they're not yours. Avoid "yes/no" questions to encourage more than one-word answers. Ask "how," "when," and "what" kinds of questions. Stay informed about and involved in their school and activities so you know what's happening during their day and have ideas of things to ask them about.

• Caring/Concern: Reassure them that you can take care of yourself and that it's your job to take care of them. Don't rely on your children to meet your emotional needs. Resist the urge to make Johnny the "man of the house, now" or have a child that is too young cooking meals or home alone. Don't suddenly encourage children to sleep with you because you're lonely. Resist the urge to share information about the divorce with them. It's an appropriate boundary that your children not have private, adult information about your marriage as well as your divorce. It's understandable that you're needy in the wake of divorce. Please turn to trusted adults to meet those needs. When you put a child in a position to take care of you, they'll feel overwhelmed by the task and they'll be put in a position to abandon their own needs. If they're taking care of you, then who's taking care of them? When you get adult support and take care of yourself, then you're in a better position to be emotionally and physically present to take care of your children.

• Tell Less, Ask More: As parents we tend to give
information, tell kids how it is and what they should or
could do. After all, we're older and (sometimes) wiser
and we want to spare our kids from harm and hardship.
However, in doing so, we often end up like the nameless,
faceless teacher from the Charlie Brown cartoons, lecturing
while all the children hear is "Whah, whah, whah, whah...."
They'll be quick to tune us out. One way we can show
loving care and concern is by listening. Ask them what they
think and how they feel. Especially be willing to ask this
periodically about how they're adjusting to the divorce.
Consider asking specifics, like how they're adjusting to
going back and forth between houses, what's on their
mind, or what feelings they've been having since they were
told about the divorce. If they don't want to talk about it,
respect that boundary and offer that you're always willing to
listen at a later time. Then, be sure you're not so busy that
you're rarely available in quiet moments (dinner, bedtime,
riding in the car, etc.) for such a conversation. This gets
back to being available. If your children notice that you're
always busy, on your phone or computer, working, watching
TV, or distracted by other things, they may not approach
you and those will be missed opportunities for conversation
and connection. (see Faber & Mazlish)

## DISCIPLINE

Imagine at your job that you have two different managers
in two different groups. You get along just fine with each of
them individually. Now imagine that after some corporate
restructuring, your job duties now involve meeting deadlines
and goals for each of these managers. However, these two
managers have entirely different agendas and management
styles. They don't communicate much with each other and
when they do, they mostly argue about who's agenda is most

important. Since they don't get very far with each other, they come to you and directly and indirectly pressure you to make their agenda your top priority, regardless of the other manager's agenda. They each demand a lot and you can't get it all done and are fearful that your year-end evaluation and possible promotions or raises are tied to the happiness of each of these managers. Can you imagine how stressed, helpless, angry, and worried you might feel? Can you imagine how you might act these frustrations out? This is your child in the middle of two parents who can't coordinate and cooperate around parenting. But worse, your child has far less power than an adult in the workplace—and no HR department with whom to air grievances—and far less maturity, life experience, and coping skills with which to navigate such a stressful situation.

Consistent rules and expectations, rewards and consequences at both homes are helpful. Entirely different rules and expectations at two different households are confusing. Inconsistency may contribute to your children being less concerned about meeting expectations because, after all, who knows what's going to happen if you don't? Your children are more likely to meet expectations when they're not confused about the limits and can predict the consequences.

You can reduce confusion by keeping rules and limits clear and consistent at both houses. Remember, it's a child's job to make their own life easier and get what they want. If he knows he can manipulate you by encouraging a popularity contest, or use guilt or the knowledge that his parents don't get along, he will. This doesn't mean he's not a good kid, it just means he's a kid and that's what they do. Effective parenting minimizes opportunities to work the system. Parents that keep each other informed and have consistent rules and consequences and are willing to back each other up reduce their children's ability to side-step limits and consequences.

# POST-DIVORCE PARENTING PITFALLS

Address these potential parenting pitfalls that can get in the way of providing consistent discipline to your children during and after divorce. Remember, it's your children's job to figure out the system that best gets them what they want with the least effort. That's not what's best for them, but it's what children do if they can get away with it. Parents teach children otherwise through caring, consistent efforts to require what's best for them. Children will find the weakness in the system (whether inconsistency, the need to be liked, competition with the other parent, guilt, or ineffective follow-through) and try to use it to get what they want. If your children are successful at this, they ultimately lose.

- **Anger or Competition with the other parent:** Your children will quickly figure out if you're willing to bend your own rules or undermine the rules agreed upon with the other parent in order to be the "fun" mom or the "nice" dad. They'll sense that you want them to like you more than their other parent. Can you see where this leads? Can you hear, "But Mom always lets me eat food in my bedroom" or "I don't have a curfew at Dad's house, he trusts me"? What might your child try to do as they get older, if they know you're hesitant to make or enforce rules so that you're not the bad guy? Is temporarily being the cool or favored parent worth the risk to your child? How might it work for them to grow up learning that they can largely do whatever they want? Your child's future boss or college professor or spouse will not have received the memo from your divorced family that they grew up learning that they could manipulate their way out of expectations and consequences. They'll be in for a rude awakening as they encounter life with others.

- **Guilt:** Many parents feel badly that their children must adjust to a divorce, so they ease up on expectations, rules, and consequences. It's understandable that you feel badly your children have suffered this loss and now have a major life adjustment to make. Don't make it worse by letting your guilty feelings cloud your parental judgment and weaken your resolve to do the hard things required of you as a parent. Your children are further abandoned when you don't hold a firm, loving line about the rules and consequences of family life. So much of what they've come to expect is changing as it is; don't also make what they understand about the rules, limits, expectations, and usual consequences for misbehavior different or inconsistent now. The most important thing related to consistency and discipline that you can do for your children during and after the divorce is to maintain the same values, rules, expectations, and consequences for them as you had while the family was intact. You cannot make up for the emotional pain your children feel because of the divorce by giving in on rules and limits. Your intention to help your children feel better is understandable; it's just that loose limits or discipline is a misplaced solution. Hold the rules and limits firmly so your children can be reassured you'll still be their parent. Instead of loosening the rules and expectations, consider adding time with your children to explore how they're doing and what they might need emotionally. You can understand their feelings without condoning misbehavior. Act on this distinction.

• **Exhaustion:** Raising children requires a lot of energy under the best of circumstances. When we're under high stress, not sleeping well, or easily distracted, it's easy to let things slide and not follow through. Single parenting is hard. You may be working more and you're solely responsible for maintaining the household as well as parenting while the children are with you. You have a lot to juggle, not to mention trying to take care of yourself. Perhaps the children are reacting emotionally or behaviorally to the divorce and presenting more parenting challenges. The temptation is high to let them stay on the Internet so you can repair the faucet instead of reminding them they've reached their limit for screen time and now need to do their chores. You could use the break, right?

Well, yes, you could, but not following through with your children makes the choice about what *you* need in that moment, not what your children need in that moment. Muster some energy, take deep breaths, and execute the limit and consequences to show your children through what you say and what you do that you're showing up consistently as their parent. Once you've done your parenting job, then take that break you need for a few moments. Use the time the children are with their other parent to truly take care of yourself and replenish your resources. I realize you're likely to be very busy and probably use some of the non-parenting time to take care of the home and errands. Please resist the urge to spend all of your non-parenting time running around until you're so exhausted so that your children return to a worn-out parent. Give yourself the best when your children aren't around so you can give your children your best when they are around. Sound difficult? It is. Difficult, but not impossible. Remember, anything of high value usually doesn't come easy and your and your children's healthy adjustment in the midst of divorce is of very high value. An investment now can pay high dividends later.

# EPILOGUE
## SEE INTO THE FUTURE AND SEE SOMETHING POSITIVE

In the midst of crisis it's often hard to see beyond our own nose, no further than what's right in front of us that day. If we do imagine the future, our vision is often fueled by the anxieties and sadness of the present, making it look bleak or catastrophic. Often, it's easy to think that how it is right now is how it will always be. It doesn't have to be and most likely won't be. You may not yet be able to imagine how your life can unfold in the years ahead—who your children will become as they grow up, what choices they'll make, who you'll become, and what choices you'll make. All I can say is that your life is not likely to remain as it is right now. You have the option to be the architect of the change you desire for yourself and your family. Imagine something positive and begin living that better life one interaction, one choice at a time, right now.

Letting go of a former life and developing a new life takes a lot of emotional energy. You need to take care of yourself, grieve the life you lost, and develop the life you want. The more you experience and resolve your feelings and invest in yourself and your new life, the less you'll remain focused on your former spouse and your old life. It's a wonderful balm and antidote to pain and resentment to invest in yourself and your future and be the best parent to your children that you can. When you take these courageous steps, you become the best example you can give to your children for managing loss and stress.

Let's face it, we parents lecture our children a lot. We have lots of advice on how to live life and what to do and what not to do. In fairness, we do want to protect our children and give them the benefit of our own experience and (hopefully) maturity. However, we all know that talk is cheap when it's just talk. Children, especially teenagers, have a keen awareness of when parents say one thing and do another. Believe me when I say that our children are paying far closer attention to our actions than to our words. If you've ever been tuned out by your child, you know this to be true.

You have a choice in how you walk through your divorce. Your children will watch how you deal with your grief and feelings, how you cope with loss, change, and stress, and how you interact with them and with their other parent. Your positive actions are teaching them—in far more powerful ways than your words—reminding them of the importance of please, thank you, respect, the golden rule, and taking care of yourself. You're teaching them by your actions how to cope with feelings, how to take care of themselves, how to manage stress and setbacks, and how to treat and respect others (especially how to treat authority figures and romantic partners).

This all may seem rather overwhelming right now. The three steps in this small book add up to one tall order. Anything truly important in this world requires effort. And big, overwhelming tasks can always be broken down into small, actionable tasks that aren't as overwhelming. One small change, one small effort, one moment of holding your tongue, one deep breath, one positive contribution, one small victory at a time builds change. Slowly, this crisis can pass, your grief can be processed and integrated into your life, and you can create new relationships and a different future.

I can give you a personal example of when I realized I was no longer so caught up in the divorce and my feelings about my children's father. I don't know exactly when the shift happened because it happened slowly and imperceptibly. But I do know that one day I just noticed I was out with a friend and I wasn't talking about him at all. We talked about all kinds of other things, but stories of slights and outrage at him wasn't part of our conversation. It felt good. And those times kept adding up. I found myself giving him credit for handling something well with the boys that was helpful to me or supportive of my parenting. I started noticing that, when I was interacting with him, I didn't have strong feelings and I wasn't distracted. I was neutral, like I was talking with one of the boys' teachers at school. It was peaceful and light, and that feeling was powerful. I wish this for you.

In the decade since the boys' dad and I divorced, we've each moved to different homes and remarried. As I mentioned, our younger son had a life-threatening accident. The boys have also had some great successes, as well as some great challenges. In that time I also lost my mother and father, the boys' grandma and grandpa. That's a lot of loss and a lot of change and adjustment for the whole family, especially a lot for two young people to navigate. I would never have imagined some of the events that came to pass after the separation. I also would never have imagined how well the boys' dad and I have been able to parent together and how cooperative we are with each other. It didn't start out that way, but over time we've both found ways to come together time and again around our children and their challenges and successes. The resources I cite and the strategies I advocate in this book are important tools that I used and deeply believe contributed to co-parenting successes.

Our sons are now teenagers. I'm proud of the young men they're becoming and I'm proud of their dad and myself for raising them well together. We've been side by side at their birthdays, sports events, school events, conferences, and medical events. We've done all that together. We've discussed their choices and hardships and deliberated consequences together. Both boys have known without a doubt that I would be checking out their stories with their dad or checking out my suspicions or intuitions with him and vise-versa—no wiggle room. I'm certain that standing united as parents has helped each of the boys as they navigated difficult teenage choices. They've also known without a doubt that we both love them very much and are there for them no matter what. It's been an enormous comfort to me to know that their dad and I are both on the same side—really the only side to be on—our children's side.

# RECOMMENDED READING

I wish you the best as you embark on the journey of navigating the divorce, your new two-household family structure, your new relationship with your co-parent, your future, and your relationship with your children. I hope this quick guide of essentials proves helpful. It's meant to provide an outline of the basic steps and skills, with brief rationale and incentive for you to make the effort, over and over again, until it doesn't take as much effort. Rome wasn't built in a day, and your divorce adjustment and effective business relationship with your co-parent won't be, either. But your consistent efforts to move you and your family in a new, positive direction will make a difference.

If you have the time, energy, or the inclination for further, more detailed information on this topic, or desire information on related topics not covered here, I recommend the following titles. I endorse these books both personally and professionally. Much of the information provided in this quick guide is discussed in more detail in the following books. I want to thank these authors for their wise and scholarly contributions referenced in this book and for their broader contribution to divorce literature, to clinicians, and to the public.

For further information on managing your own emotions and

processing the loss of the divorce, read Gold. If you desire specific information on the divorce process, such as non-combative options for divorcing, how to talk to children about divorce, and parenting plan options, read Emery and Gold.

For a good summary of the effects of divorce on children and what is most important for children's adjustment, read Emery.

"The Children's Bill of Rights in Divorce" pg. 82 Emery

"The Seven Keys to a Healthy Divorce" pg. 49 Gold

"Summary of Basic Ground Rules for Parenting Successfully" pg. 125 Gold

"A Dozen Golden Parent Agreement Rules" pg. 72–80 Thayer & Zimmerman

For more in depth review of communication skills and effective negotiation, read Stone, Patton, & Heen. Also read Gold for handling conflict and negotiation specific to divorce.

More detailed and excellent information on working well with the other parent is available in Emery, Gold, Ross & Corcoran, and Thayer & Zimmerman.

As the title suggests, if you do not believe you will be able to work cooperatively with the other parent, but still want to offer your best effort at co-parenting to your children, read Ross & Corcoran and Thayer & Zimmerman.

For general information and great guidance on parenting, read Gottman, Cline & Fay, and Faber & Mazlish.

# REFERENCES

Cline, F. & Fay, J. (2006). Parenting with Love and Logic

Emery, R.E. PhD (2004). The Truth About Children and Divorce

Faber, A. & Mazlish, E. (2012). How To Talk So Kids Will Listen & Listen So Kids Will Talk

Gold, L. MSW (2009). The Healthy Divorce

Gottman, J. Ph.D. (1998). Raising An Emotionally Intelligent Child The Heart of Parenting

Ross, J.A. & Corcoran, J. (1996) Joint Custody with a Jerk: Raising a Child with an Uncooperative Ex

Stone, Patton, & Heen (1999). Difficult Conversations

Thayer & Zimmerman (2001). The Co-Parenting Survival Guide

# NOTES

Made in the USA
San Bernardino, CA
14 May 2019